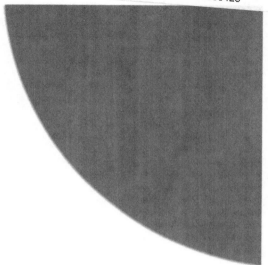

Face-To-Face Networking

It's All About Communication

KATHY CONDON

Face-To-Face Networking:

It's All About Communication

Kathy@kathycondon.info
(360) 695-4313
5535 E. Evergreen Blvd., #7102
Vancouver, Washington 98661

Library of Congress Cataloging-in-Publication Data:
Condon, Kathy
Face-To-Face Networking It's All About Communication
/Kathy Condon
ISBN 978-0-9815941-1-8
Printed in the United States of America

Table of Contents

v |

DEDICATION

THIS BOOK IS DEDICATED TO:

Mrs. Mora Jensen

The dedication of a book is something that I do not take lightly. My first book: **It Doesn't Hurt to Ask: It's All About Communication** was dedicated to my parents, Alma and Francis Hellmich. There is no question they gave me a solid foundation for my beliefs and values that have sustained me throughout my life.

 I attended a one-room school located in rural Wisconsin, 11 miles outside the town of Tomah. Our school had 27 students. Mrs. Jensen taught all eight grades and all subjects.

She was my teacher for six years--grades one through six. She retired at the end of my sixth grade. There was rarely a time that she did not smile.

About five years ago, I went to visit Mrs. Jensen, who now was in her early nineties. When she greeted my mom and me at the door, she had that same contagious smile. The next hour was filled with reminiscing about life then. It was a time when all the families in the school knew each other well and when I had outstanding penmanship.

Mrs. Jensen has since passed on. Fortunately, I do not have to say, "I wish I would have gone to see her and thanked her for kindness and her wisdom." I told her that in person. Mrs. Jensen not only believed in me, she supported me through the challenges we experienced as a family, and she stretched me.

Thus, this book is dedicated to Mrs. Jensen, a woman with a contagious smile and a desire to help all with whom she came in contact. May the world have many teachers like Mrs. Jensen.

Introduction:

I have taught face-to-face networking for years. Yet people continue to have the same, basic questions. Thus, I believe it is time that I share with you what I know about face-to-face networking. There is nothing here that I do not do myself.

Let me begin by saying face-to-face networking skills are the same, whether you use them to build personal or business interactions. People working in non-profit organizations, churches or schools need to learn face-to-face networking skills. Introverts and extroverts need to learn face-to-face networking skills too. There are tools you need and skills to be honed, yet face-to-face networking is not out of the reach any person.

What Will You Discover When You Read This Book?

The tools for face-to-face networking are easy to obtain. The skills can be practiced as you go about your daily life. In fact, each time you start a conversation with a person, you are networking. Each person you come in contact with is part of your network.

Each chapter is complete in and of itself. You can go to the subject that is causing you concern and find simple techniques that will help you.

What About Social Media? Isn't It Making Face-to Face Networking Obsolete?

The initial wave of people believing social media would be the ideal and only way to connect with people has passed. Now people realize that face-to-face networking remains an effective way to connect with others, and needs to be part of your marketing plan.

I believe in social media networking. In fact, I am one of the early users. I make sure I log on to sites and add at least one comment or ask a question each day. Yet, I find that when I meet face-to-face with one of my contacts over a cup of coffee ideas flow easily and relationships continue to strengthen.

Social media users are forming groups. They find a place that has Wi-Fi and invite people to come and meet them in person. It is there that face-to-face networking skills come into play. These networking events are no different from others. People arrange to meet with each other at another time and place in order to get know the people they meet at the event even better.

My belief is that face-to-face networking will never go out of style. It is needed now more than ever. People need to be acknowledged and made to feel that they are important or significant in this world. A handshake, a handwritten note, or a phone call today has a much larger impact then it has in the past. Technology will continue to be used, but these simple, personal actions truly make a person feel special because it is just for him or her.

If you learned the tools included in this book long ago, it is time to dust them off once again. If you were never taught the tools and skills to do face-to-face networking, this book is for you too.

A toast to your next face-to-face networking event: "May you learn something and have fun."

1

Want to be Remembered? Have a Great Handshake

"What makes a great handshake?"

 It is interesting that handshakes, like politics and religion, are rarely discussed openly. However, weak, wimpy handshakes are talked about in whispers.

Like it or not, you create an impression with your handshake. A wimpy handshake sends immediate thoughts to the receiver that this person is not very self-assured. I know it may not be fair. However, perception is reality.

Through the years, I have discovered a number of things regarding handshakes that I believe you will find of interest. Let me share with you some stories that illustrate why we need to pay much more attention to this important networking tool.

Example 1:

I was selected to make a presentation for a Chamber of Commerce luncheon on networking. While I was preparing the presentation, I thought of a CEO who I was confident would be attending. He had a terrible handshake—wimpy to say the least. With that in mind, I decided to add ***"How to Shake Hands"*** into my presentation.

Once I looked over the crowd, I realized that the man, who was my intended target for the discussion of handshakes, was not there. I decided to go ahead with my presentation as I had designed it.

I brought one of the attendees to the front of the room. We then proceeded to illustrate the proper way to shake hands. Interactive participation is the hallmark of my presentations, so I directed people to shake hands with three people.

At the end of my presentation, a number of people asked questions about handshakes. While driving home, I realized people obviously wanted to learn more about this subject.

Example 2:

I was asked to do an icebreaker for a meeting at my Rotary Club. After thinking it over, I determined that a good icebreaker topic would be "***How to Shake Hands.***" The Rotary Club president looked at me in disbelief. "You are going to teach these successful business people about handshakes?" he exclaimed. I replied, "Yes, I am."

At the meeting, I asked a volunteer to come to the front of the room. We shook hands. Much to his relief, I said, "Great handshake." My volunteer and I proceeded to illustrate to the audience "why" the handshake was appropriate and good. Then my fellow Rotarians were asked to share handshakes with five people in the room. The energy in the room soared as they practiced their handshakes.

At the end of the meeting, six Rotarians approached me with questions about handshakes.

This presentation made it evident to me that not only did people not know how to give a proper handshake; they wanted to learn the appropriate way to create a good impression through a handshake. I needed to build this exercise into all of my trainings.

WHEN IS SHAKING HANDS APPROPRIATE?

My flippant answer would be 'all the time.' On the other hand, perhaps it is not such a flippant answer. When we extend our hand with a smile, the other person's face lights up for you are making that person feel significant or important. At that moment, he or she is the most important person in the world to you and he feels it.

Does this sound a little overly dramatic? I think not. This underutilized gesture of shaking hands actually needs to be used more. Since this chapter is about shaking hands and doing business in the United States, let's look at some specific times when it is correct to shake hands and take advantage of some outstanding opportunities to connect with people.

HELPFUL SHAKING HANDS ETIQUETTE

- Men have been taught to wait to see if a woman is going to extend her hand. They tell me that it is often awkward meeting a woman for the first time because they do not know if she will want to shake hands with them.

  When approaching a man or woman, immediately extend your hand so there is no question about your desire to shake hands.

- You are seated at a table and a good friend comes over to introduce you to his colleague.

  If you are a man or woman, stand up and shake hands with the person. Please note I said man or woman. Why should a woman remain seated and reach up her hand?

- You are introduced to someone who is blind. There is no way he will have any idea that you want to shake hands with him. You say, "I would like to shake your hand." Watch the smile emerge on the recipient's face.

- A person enters the room in a wheelchair. You may or may not know him.

  Extend your hand and shake hands with him. A person in a wheelchair once told me that people rarely ask him to shake hands—he looked so sad when he told me.

- You walk into an interview and there is a panel of five people. Shake hands with each person before you sit down. You will stand out from the other candidates.

WHAT MAKES A GOOD HANDSHAKE?

1. When the Vs of each other's hands touch (space between your thumb and forefinger).

2. When the grasp is firm and a couple of up and down pumps are made.

3. When both people look each other in the eye and smile while you shake hands.

My belief is that it is important for parents to make sure that their children know how to give a firm handshake. It is never too early to start teaching our children this valuable social skill. Shaking hands may be discussed in our classrooms. However, my experience is that there are way too many wimpy handshakes, so it is time to take this important networking tool seriously.

How is your handshake?

IT'S THE LITTLE THINGS

1. Etiquette rules for shaking hands are the same for men and women.

2. Make sure you teach your children and employees how to give a handshake that makes a positive impression.

3. Give handshakes often and keep them strong.

Notes

2

Contact Cards, Not Business Cards

"Why are they called contact cards, and what do you put on them?"

Last week my sister gave me a bad time because I corrected her when she said business card. She said, "Kathleen, when are you going to give up on your crusade to change the name of business cards to contacts cards?" I replied, "I'm not!"

A little background is required here. When I was doing three-day workshops for people making a career transition, the need to have business cards for your job search was addressed. When I asked attendees how many of them had business cards, no one raised their hand. I remembered one of the participants said to me, "Kathy, that is why we are here, we don't have a card because we are not employed so we have nothing to put on it."

Therein lays the problem. People didn't have a card because they thought they had to include the name of a business in order to carry this all-important piece of paper. Since I was teaching a class of 14 people about how to find jobs, I explained the issue. "It seems to me we have the wrong name for this piece of paper, but I do not know what it should be called. Calling card seems too old-fashioned." I challenged the class to come up with a new name for it.

The next day, as class began, a young man raised his hand. He said, "Kathy, I have a name for the card. It is a contact card." We all looked at each other...duh.....of course, that's it—a contact card! For it has our contact information on it. From that moment on, I have referred to a 2-inch by 3.5-inch piece of paper as a contact card.

WHAT DO YOU PUT ON A CONTACT CARD?

Name

Phone Number

Physical Address (More on that later)

Email Address

Website

Personally, I have decided not to add a link to any of
my social media site addresses on my contact card—
one never knows when sites may go out of business or
are bought out.

What Is Missing from the Card?

1. I do not believe in putting a position title on it if
   you are looking for a new job for two reasons:

   a. Companies do not use the same title for
      similar positions. Example: Salesperson in one
      company could be called an Account
      Representative or Business Development
      Director in another.

   b. After the Hiring Manager interviews you, he
      may feel that there is an entirely different
      position that might match your skills. You

want to make sure you keep all of your
options open.

2. After looking at thousands of cards, I can tell you
the trend is not to put your picture on it unless you
are a real estate agent.

3. I had the experience of having a card with writing
on the back. It was soooo frustrating for there
literally was no place to write a note on the card
to make reminders to myself or add information
for the person I was handing it to. My
recommendation is, leave the back of the card
blank.

4. Contacts cards with a plastic coating on them look
great. You love them UNTIL you try to write
something on them. My one experience with
plastic coated contact cards proved to me that the
chances are slim to none that you will have a pen
with you that will work to write that note on it.

My recommendation: Coat only the front side of
your contact card.

5. Social media links: Since technology is changing
    so quickly, I am refraining from making a
    recommendation about which links to put on your
    card, though the trend is to include them.

*Why should you put your physical address on your
contact card?*

Why do I recommend the address? More than once, I
have been frustrated when I looked at a contact card
and found no mailing address. There is the name,
phone number, email address, and website. Yet, there
I am sitting with pen in hand ready to write a
handwritten note and I have to go back to the
computer, go to the website, and "hope" that I can
find a physical address.

If you are worrying about security, seriously consider a post office box. If you have a home office, it just might be a welcome relief to separate your office and personal mail. By providing your mailing address, you are helping make it easy for people to contact you. Then you might just be the recipient of a handwritten note, which will surely bring a smile to your face when you open up your mailbox.

IT'S THE LITTLE THINGS

1. A contact card is essential—get one that you are proud to give out.

2. Make sure you ALWAYS have contact cards with you—you never know when you might have a need for one.

I recently went to a garage sale and totally connected with the woman who was having the sale. I actually, got in the car, thought about it, went back, gave her my contact card, and asked if we could have coffee. She was delighted.

3. My view? The contact card is one of the most important communication tools that exist. It helps us connects with the people in our world.

3

Do You Really Need A Nametag?

"On which side should you wear your

nametag?"

You enter the hallway where you will be attending an event. The first stop is the reservation desk. You give your name. Someone checks off your name from a list. Then one of two things happens:

1. "They say we have your nametag over there." Heaven forbid if it is sitting there waiting for you.

If they have preprinted your nametag, I am fairly certain the nametag will include their logo, which will take up one—third of the space of the nametag. Your name will be in capital letters and then the following line will include your company name. If you are at a convention, it will more than likely, include your home city and state. Try to read this information from a distance.

Oh yes, your nametag will more than likely be the sticky variety. This kind of nametags cause havoc on anything that smacks of suede or leather. If the organization has gone the economy route with the nametags, you can be pretty assured that it will curl up or fall off during the course of the event.

If your nametag is put on one of those long cords, the chances of it being face out when you really need it available are about 75%. Now let's talk about the length of the cord. Do you really want people looking down at your bust or stomach?

I have attended hundreds of networking events. I can honestly say I have received a readable preprinted nametag about 5% of the time. When I do, I make sure I compliment the organizers of the event.

2.   *The people at the reservation desk direct you to a line to make out your own nametag.*

You dutifully go to the end of the line and watch as a person picks up a marker and writes his name and company name on a blank nametag. It is not unusual to see a line six people deep at the nametag station, for the organizers have forgotten to bring extra markers.

Once someone has filled out a nametag, it is interesting to note how he continues to just stand there before he picks up the nametag, peels the back off, and puts it on his shoulder. Then he finally moves out of line. It is not an exaggeration to say that one can lose five minutes of networking time standing in line waiting to get a nametag.

PERMANENT NAMETAGS MAKE YOUR LIFE EASIER

Frustrated with the two scenarios above, I knew there had to be another way. I personally, began the process of finding the perfect nametag—one that I would carry with me at all times and be proud to wear. My rationale was that it would be readable AND end the days of standing in line making out my nametag.

I started with one that ended up looking like a billboard. Way too big—all it needed was a flashing neon light. That didn't work.

Then there was the metal one with my name written in metallic letters. A teenager said to me "That is a really ugly nametag." So that nametag was quickly relegated to the recycling box.

After four aborted efforts, I have found the perfect combination. One that is dignified and readable from a distance. It is 3 inch by 1.5-inch high oval. The background is dark navy and my name is in white letters. Perfect. Readable from a distance. Since oval shaped nametags are unusual, they are not easy to find. However, I have discovered companies, that make plaques, are happy to make nametags according to your specifications.

In addition, my nametag has a strong magnet on the back. Not only is it strong enough to hold through lapels on my jackets, it works perfectly with silk blouses. No more worrying about whether pins will wreck the fabric of my clothing or fearing the nametag would fall off.

The only information I include on my customized nametag is my name. Networking is about building relationships. People do business with people they know and like. Get to know the person standing before you. See Chapter 8 on how to start and maintain a conversation.

At a networking event, you want to make sure you make it easy for the person to remember you. Your name in clear print is a great visual tool to reinforce your name. In addition, if someone comes up to the person you are talking with, it makes it easy for the other person to introduce you by name to the late arrival.

And let's not forget the times when you are talking with someone whom you have known for years and for the life of you, you cannot remember his or her name. Do you think a clear nametag on the other person would come in handy then?

WHICH SIDE SHOULD YOU WEAR YOUR NAMETAG?

Scott Ginsberg has become famous for wearing his nametag "Scott", 24 hours a day. He even has a tattoo on his chest in the form of a nametag with the word, "Scott." He and I have had a running friendly rivalry for years about which shoulder is the correct side to wear a nametag. Scott says the left and I'm a strong advocate for the right.

Scott believes that when you are walking down the street, you want people to easily read your nametag so you have it on the left. My view, I am wearing my nametag at networking events so the right side works better.

Politicians and fundraisers were some of the first to recognize that with the nametag on the right, it is easy to see when you are shaking hands with a person. Yes,

I know some people are left-handed and it isn't quite
as handy. For the majority of us, however, by placing
our nametag on our right shoulder we are making it
easy for the person to see our name.

So there's my reasoning and I'm sticking to it.

KEEP YOUR NAMETAG WITH YOU AT ALL TIMES

I recommend that you purchase at least three
nametags at the same time. Personally, I keep one in
my car, one in my purse and one in my training
materials bag. You never know when you are going to
have a use for it.

Admittedly, I took a little teasing from some of the executives in my community at first. They said, "Wow, Kathy has come far in this world, she has her own nametag now." After the first time they saw it, they started making comments about what a good idea it was to have my own nametag.

One day, I was at a big community event. I went up to the editor of my local newspaper and extended my hand. Before I could get my name out, I saw him looking at my nametag and said "Kathy, great to see you again." Inside I smiled for I knew I had prevented his embarrassment by having my name so readily available.

Let's face it: You know your name—make it easy for people to remember yours.

IT'S THE LITTLE THINGS

1. A nametag is one of the most important tools you need for networking.

2. Make sure your name is easily readable from a distance.

3. Nametags are not about advertising you—it is about making it easy for the people with whom you come in contact at networking events.

4

How Do You Find a Place to Network?

"What criteria works for selecting networking events?"

It would be pointless for me to write a book about face-to-face networking if I didn't help you find places to network. Let me give you some examples that illustrate how easy it is to find places to make new connections or strengthen the connections you have already made.

Example 1:

I was driving from Vancouver, Washington to Palm Springs, California to housesit. On the way down, I stopped at a restaurant. I walked in and took a seat at the classy bar. It was supposed to be a quick stop and I was alone.

Before I had ordered, a man sat down next to me and we began to talk. He was on his way to San Francisco to a tradeshow to display and sell his special brand of Belgium chocolate.

After we had eaten, it was time for both us to continue our separate journeys. We exchanged contact cards. I traded my book "*It Doesn't Hurt to Ask: It's All About Communication*" for some tins of his chocolate.

Once I was at my destination, we exchanged a few emails—both of us commenting on each other's product. However, what was even more interesting about our email exchange, I received an email from a consultant named Susan who was working in Palm Springs. She said her friend, the same man I met at the restaurant, had given her my information for he thought we should meet.

Susan and I met and lamented that we had not met before so we could have spent more time together exploring the Coachella Valley. It is now one year later, and we regularly communicate with each other. This is the perfect example of why you need to follow up after you have met a person for the first time.

Example 2:

I was visiting Palm Springs and I was reading the local newspaper. In the paper, there was an excellent article written by executive coach, Nancy Laura Joseph. At the end of the column there was only her name, so I Googled her name and found her contact information.

Since my time was short in Palm Springs, I sent Nancy an email (normally, I would have sent her a handwritten note) introducing myself. I commented on her article and asked her if we could get together for a cup of coffee. A reply came back quickly.

We set up a coffee date and had a delightful two hours together. We had an authentic conversation filled with "ahas." Now we are connected and both of us feel free to get in touch with each other when we want to bounce an idea off someone.

You may meet someone in a grocery store line. You start talking while you are waiting. Before long, you realize there is a way you are connected or how you

can help each other. This is why it is important to
have your contact cards with you at all times.

THE INTERNET CAN RECONNECT US

Many of us have lost contact with people who we
were acquainted with in the past. It may be a former
classmate, a colleague, a person you met at a
conference or a neighbor who lived next-door years
ago. I encourage you to search for the person. Email
or call him and remind him who you are and start up a
conversation.

Invite the person for coffee if he is still in your
community. If he lives in a distant town or state, make
a note where he is located. Next time you are going to
be in his town, give him a call and see if you can get
together face-to-face.

Do not worry about how long it has been since you
connected. Wouldn't you be flattered if someone
remembered you and got in touch after five years? It
is never too late to get in touch with a person—even if
it has been a number of years.

READ LOCAL PUBLICATIONS

The next time you enter your local coffee shop, look
around for some of the leaflets and small publications
that are available. Often these publications contain a
calendar of events. Remember all events are
networking events.

People seem to take great delight in telling me that
they do not read the newspaper. Then they wonder
why it is so hard to carry on conversations when they
meet people. There is nothing better than mentioning

to a person who has just received a positive accolade that you saw it in the newspaper or online.

A bonus tip: Send the article or link to the person with a note and your contact card.

In addition to articles about people, you will find ads in the newspaper and online that highlight upcoming events. Often an event is found within a company's regular ad for they support non-profits by including information on their fundraisers. Make sure you glance at the ads as you breeze through the papers or check online sites.

GROUND BREAKING CEREMONIES

One of my favorite places to network is a groundbreaking ceremony. Think about it, no groundbreaking ceremony happens without the top management of the company and the community leaders attending. Invariably, the event starts late. While waiting for the festivities to begin, you may find yourself standing next to the company's head of public relations or its human resources director.

It is easy to start a conversation with the person next to you when you know you are all there for the same purpose—welcoming a new addition to the community. If it is an employee of the company, ask him or her questions about the company. Learn as much as you can.

After the ceremony is over, shake hands with the person you connected with and say, "Do you have a contact card?" Then you can say, "I enjoyed our conversation and appreciate you sharing information about the company."

Alternatively, if the employee is a transplant to the area, offer to have coffee with him or her and share more information about your community.

Follow up by sending the person you met a
handwritten note. You now have a "friend" within the
company. Even if you are not sure why you need it,
you have the contact information. You never know
when someone you know might need an introduction
to someone within the company.

RIBBON CUTTING CEREMONIES

Ribbon cuttings are my least favorite events to go to
for networking. Normally, there are large crowds.
Especially if it is a smaller building, one can find
herself shoulder to shoulder with people.

If there is food, the situation gets more precarious for
there is a chance someone's drink balanced on his
plate can end up down the front of you. At such an
event, I had a glass of wine dumped all the way down
the front of my turquoise top. Not only was I a mess,
the top was ruined—now I wear dark colored tops
when I expect that there will be a crowd at an event.

Since it is crowded, and many people have come for
the food, I find this environment is not conducive to
the conversations that I suggest in Chapter 8. My
preference is to avoid ribbon cuttings. Instead, I send a
handwritten note to congratulate the owners on their
new location and welcome them to the community,
and of course, include my contact card.

CIVIC EVENTS BRING OUT THE MOVERS AND SHAKERS

One of the not to be missed events in my city is the
State of the City Address given by our mayor. Often
this event is free, or a nominal fee of $5 to help pay
for the coffee and rolls that are served. Another event
not to be missed is the State of the County Address
delivered by the current Chair of the County Board of
Supervisors.

The key to attending events such as these is to make
sure you arrive early. It gives you time to talk with
people before the presentation is made. Keep in mind
that after an event people rarely stick around and talk.

MAILING LISTS KEEP YOU INFORMED

If there is a guest book at an event you are attending,
make sure you sign it with your name and address.
Then you will be sure to receive invitations in the mail
for events in the future.

If you are serious about networking, your goal should
be to get on mailing lists, NOT keeping your name off
lists. Through mailing lists, you find out what is
happening in your community.

FUNDRAISERS LEVEL THE PLAYING FIELD

Fundraisers level the playing field. What do I mean?

Let's use an example of a fundraiser for the Humane
Society. Now think about it. A CEO has a dog, you
have a dog, and the woman that lives next to you has a
cat. You all decide you are going to help support your
local Humane Society, so you sign up to come to the
event.

Now it is time for dinner and you find your way to a
table and take a seat next to a woman. You have no
idea what she does professionally. You assume she is
there because she loves animals. There is a 99 percent
chance you are right in your thinking.

Imagine how easy it is start a conversation. You ask,
"What kind of animal do you have?" You watch her

smile as she replies and starts talking about her
beloved pet. Listen closely to how she answers your
question. Something she says will more than likely
trigger an idea for another question you can ask her.

Remember you know everything you know; you want
to learn something new.

At the end of the evening, as you are shaking hands
and telling her goodnight, ask her if she has a contact
card. Once you look at the card, you realize that you
have been talking to a president of a large corporation
in your area. Fundraisers are great, for they take the
pressure off everyone. You are there to have fun and
support a cause you believe in—your position in the
community does not matter.

Now as a reminder—make sure you send a
handwritten note after the event (See Chapter 10 for
details on what to say in the note).

CRITERIA I USE FOR SELECTING WHICH EVENTS TO ATTEND

Since there are hundreds of opportunities to meet new people each month, I need a way to sort through the abundance of events and decide which ones I want to add to my calendar.

Here's my solution. I ask myself:

1. Will I learn something?

2. Will I have fun?

If I answer 'yes' to either of these two questions, the event is placed on my calendar and a reservation is made (See Chapter 5).

Instead of dreading going to an event, think about
what you will learn or how much fun you are going to
have. You know you have selected well when you
leave the event and there is a smile on your face and
spring in your step.

IT'S THE LITTLE THINGS

1. After you meet a person, make sure you follow up
    with them. Write a note or call them.

2. Decide which events you are going to go to by
    asking: Will I learn something? Or will I have
    fun?

3. Even if it has been years since you connected with
    someone, do it anyway. Think about it, wouldn't
    you be pleased if someone remembered you after
    a number of years?

Want to be Remembered? Make Sure You RSVP

"Why is it important to make a reservation?"

The term RSVP comes from the French expression "répondez s'il vous plaît", meaning, "please respond."

I lived on the East Coast for four years. One of the things I learned was that no one would ever consider showing up to an event if she had not notified the host that she was coming. It didn't matter how formal the event, you let the host know your intentions to attend or not to attend.

A move to the Northwest and my role as Executive Director of Columbia Arts Center brought a new perspective to the importance of the RSVP. Invitations were send out for a special event. About 25 people indicated they were coming so the staff planned accordingly. Food was ordered and handouts were made. At the night of the event, people who hadn't bothered to RSVP showed up. People kept flowing through the door. In the end, the count for the evening came to 45 people, nearly twice as many as we had planned for.

The next event was a gala event opening during the winter holiday season. Invitations were sent and 75 people responded that they would be attending. Staff planned for 75 people, plus about 25 extra. Over 150 people walked through the door in their holiday finery. Needless to say, there was a real flurry in the kitchen and quiet trips to the store by the staff for more food.

What was the issue? People in the Northwest tend not to make reservations. We can attribute this to the free spirit of people in the Northwest who do not want to make plans too far ahead of time. Or we can believe, as I do, that they are not aware why it is important to RSVP.

Frustrated after seeing the same phenomena happen over again, I realized I had to come up with a way to explain to people in my networking seminars why it was important to RSVP.

WHY YOU SHOULD RSVP

I learned long ago that what seems obvious to me is not obvious to others. Perhaps, one has to be in charge of an event to really understand the inconvenience to the host when someone doesn't RSVP. Or if you have ever planned a wedding and each person attending will cost you a minimum of $25 you know how important an exact count is to your budget.

The same is true for any kind of event. Often there is a need for nametags (have you priced them recently?), handouts and, of course, the all-important snack that is served at a break. Funds are required. If you are on a non-profit board, you understand how difficult it is for non-profits to meet their goals and every cent becomes a factor.

You get the picture—your lack of attention to answering an RSVP can cost people money. Even more importantly, you are missing out on an outstanding way to be remembered.

Let me explain:

- When you make your RSVP, your name goes on a list.

- Two weeks out the people in charge will look at the list—your name is there.

- One week out people look at the list—your name is there.

- Two days out people look at the list—your name is there.

- The day of the event the list is printed out—your name is there.

- A nametag is printed for you—your name is on one.

- At the registration desk, you check in—your name is there.

- If there is a speaker, often the list will be printed out for her—your name is there.

- After the event, a list of attendees is created—your name is there.

Now let's contrast this with showing up without a RSVP:

- You walk up to the registration desk and apologize because you had not made an RSVP. Positive first impression? I think not.

- You hand them your cash.

- You write out your own nametag.

- Someone takes your cash. They do not ask your name. When the attendee list is updated, your name does not appear on the attendee list.

Convinced of the importance of RSVPs?

Think of this way, when you make a RSVP your name
is noted and looked at nine times. When you just walk
in, there is a strong possibility that your name will not
even be recorded as an attendee.

IT'S THE LITTLE THINGS

1. Show respect to the host—reply promptly to an
   RSVP request.

2. The quicker you RSVP, the more opportunities
   you have for your name to be seen and
   remembered.

3. To really be remembered, send a handwritten thank you card after the event with your contact card included. Handwritten notes are rare and they are appreciated.

6

You are Ready to Walk into a Room Full of Strangers. Now What?

"How do you decide whom to approach?"

 My recommendation is that you do not go with a friend or colleague to a networking event. If you do, make a pact that you will split up and not spend all your time with each other. You already know each others' stories. If it is a colleague, use the water cooler at work to discuss the latest happenings in your office. You are here to meet new people.

You have checked in at the reservation desk and have your nametag on your shoulder. Now it is time for you to walk into the networking event.

As you go through the door, you may be thinking: "I hate these events." "Wish I would have brought Harry with me." "Wonder if they have some good food." "Think I'll head right to the bar." "I'm an introvert, why in the world do I put myself into these situations?"

Sound familiar? You do not have the corner on these thoughts—there is not a person alive who does not feel some sort of trepidation as he enters a room full of strangers. So do not be hard on yourself.

WHAT DO YOU DO WHEN YOU WALK INTO A ROOM?

Move to the right of the door. I have discovered an interesting phenomenon. To the right of the door there is never a coat rack, people, or a food table. There may be a plant and occasionally a garbage can. However, there will be a place for you to stand. Take a few deep breathes and look over the assembled group.

What are you looking for?

The person standing alone. I know you have experienced being at an event and finding yourself standing alone. You are wondering what you should do next. Or even worse, you are thinking to yourself "I'm such a loser, no one wants to talk to me." I trust you are smiling; now you know others have been subjected to the same fate.

If you were the one standing all alone, wouldn't you be happy to have someone approach you with a smile and a handshake as she said her name? Of course, you would. I'm betting in return she will smile and give you a firm handshake back.

What if the person is standing all alone because he is a real loser and people are avoiding him for a reason?

I would caution you to eliminate that way of thinking. Let me give you some examples of when I met some outstanding people who were standing all alone.

Example 1:

I journeyed to a distant city to hear a prominent person make a major address during a formal dinner.

My goal was to attend the dinner only and skip the cocktail hour for I would know no one in the room.

At the registration desk, I learned that the speaker had been delayed, so everything had been moved back and the cocktail hour was now just getting into full swing. My immediate thought was "I think I will go check out the bookstore I saw down the street." This was a perfect example, of my own fear of entering a room full of strangers rearing its' head.

Then I caught myself, "Kathy, you teach this stuff—go to the cocktail party." I went up the stairs, walked into the room and stood to the right of the door. In the far corner, I saw a man in his early 80s standing by himself.

I approached the man with my hand reached out and said, "Hi, I'm Kathy Condon. What great thing

happened to you recently?" (More about this question
in Chapter 8) He returned the handshake, smiled, and
said, "I guess it happened this morning." I replied,
"And what was that great thing?" He said, "Well I was
talking to the President of the United States this
morning about how to save the streams in the
Northwest."

Needless to say, I was taken back. I regained my
composure and proceeded to have one of the most
interesting conversations I have had in a long time. I
broke my own rule that night and spent most of the
hour talking to him instead of trying to connect with
other people.

Remember, this was the man standing all alone. Was
he interesting, important and worth getting to know?
You bet.

59 | Y o u   a r e   R e a d y   t o   W a l k   i n t o   a
R o o m   F u l l   o f   S t r a n g e r s .   N o w
W h a t ?

Example 2:

Those of us who train or speak at functions often find ourselves in the back of the room standing all alone. People do not know who we are so they continue their conversations with other participants and avoid interaction with the newcomers.

The perfect time to connect with a person with a speaker or trainer before an event. In fact, I encourage people to go up to speakers and trainers before the event starts to introduce themselves. It may be the only time to connect personally and it gives the speaker or trainer a friendly face to connect with as they deliver their presentation.

Do not worry about interrupting the person while they are setting up. If the person is not prepared before you walked into the room, you have selected the wrong person to present. We are prepared. We are nervous too. Actually, we are usually just fussing with papers to make it look like we are busy. Come up and introduce yourself.

Example 3:

I was at a fundraiser for an art museum. There was a lovely looking woman standing all alone. I went up to her, extended my hand, and gave her my name. I was greeted with a terrific smile and I learned that she was the curator of the exhibit we were viewing. I had been hearing such good things about her.

Our conversation continued that evening and, before I knew it, she had agreed to come to speak to Rotary about the exhibit with art from Greece. I was honored to be the one to introduce her to my fellow Rotarians when she shared information about the art exhibit. It would not have happened if I had not gone up to the person standing all alone.

HOW CAN YOU MAKE YOURSELF MISERABLE AT AN EVENT?

Keep trying to break into a conversation when two people are facing each other. When two people are facing each other, they are in what we call rapport. They are interested in what the other has to say and they are exchanging information. They do not want to be interrupted. They do not want to welcome another person into the conversation.

Think of it this way. If you hadn't seen a fellow classmate in 15 years, and you ran into each other event with only 10 minutes to talk, would you want someone else joining into the conversation? I think not.

IF YOU CANNOT FIND A PERSON STANDING ALL ALONE, WHAT CAN YOU DO?

Look for two people who are standing side-by-side facing out toward the crowd. More than likely, they have run out of things to talk about. They are hoping someone saves them for they have not figured out how to move out of a conversation.

I have discovered when people are bored at an event, a woman will start fussing with something in her hand,—it might be a napkin, a glass, or even a paper clip that she has picked up. The man will invariably put his hand in his pocket and lean on one leg. If you don't believe me, check out the phenomena at the next event you attend.

When two people are facing out, it is easy for you to go up to them, extend your hand and say your name.

Trust me; you will not only be welcomed you will immediately be drawn into the conversation.

ENTERING A CIRCLE OF PEOPLE

This technique works, though it might take time for you find the right time to jump in and make an appropriate comment. If you are joining a circle, do not interrupt the conversation by shaking hands and giving your name. You are a bystander until someone in the group sees fit to draw you into the conversation.

IT'S THE LITTLE THINGS

1. The easiest way to begin networking in a room is look for the person standing alone.

2. The second easiest way to begin a conversation is look for two people facing out toward the assembled crowd.

3. The way to make yourself miserable at an event is try to break into conversations where two people are facing each other and obviously engaged in a conversation.

7

You Need to Meet People at This Event, Now What?

"When should you arrive at an event and why?"

You have decided on this particular event because you know you either will learn something or will have fun. My guess is that, more than likely, you will do both each time you go out.

Let us start with a few basic steps:

YOUR ARRIVAL TIME

Most events have listed the actual start time of the formal program in their advertising material. It might say, "Doors open at 8:00 a.m. with formal presentation to begin at 9:00 a.m." If that is the case, you know there is time to mingle with the other participants.

Yes, I know some of you are thinking I would arrive at 8:45 a.m. and go straight to my table. Let me say, I believe that is one of the biggest mistakes you can make if you are serious about meeting new people.

Recently, I signed up to attend a public relations meeting early in the morning. Following my own

advice, I arrived three-quarters of an hour early. I walked into the room full of public relations people.

WHAT DID I NOTICE?

The room was very quiet. Feeling this was very odd for a room full of public relations professionals; I stepped to the right of the door and observed what was happening. Here is what I noticed:

1. Even though it was three-quarters of an hour before the formal presentation was to begin, all of the attendees had gone to the buffet table, filled their plates, and took their meals to their tables.

Hint: When you immediately head to the food table, you limit your chances of meeting many new people.

You will be stuck with the person you sat down next to for the duration of the event.

2. It was easy to verify that people were sitting with
    their own colleagues because they all had
    nametags. One can only imagine the conversation
    that went on about the latest budget report, who
    just got a pink slip, or who was recently hired; all
    information that would have been easily captured
    at the workplace.

*Hint: Make a pact with your colleagues that you will
all sit at different tables. The advantage is that you
will all learn different things, you will be able to
share information about your company, and you will
double, at a minimum, the number of people your
team meets.*

3. Once people were done with their meals, they
    started fussing with their smart phones. There they
    were with their heads looking down into their
    laps. They were texting instead of getting up out
    of their chairs and talking with people face-to-
    face.

Hint: Turn the sound off on your smart phone as you enter a room. You don't have to worry about it ringing in the middle of a conversation.

The room was filling quickly, so I looked for a table where my seat would be facing the podium. I looked for a seat that was beside someone who appeared to be interesting and that I had never met. My goal was to learn something new and meet new people.

I approached the table and asked if this seat was available. Love it when the person says, "Yes, I'm saving it just for you." I know that kind of comment sounds trite, but it started the conversation on a high note. Then I smiled, introduced myself, and set my

briefcase down. It was still very early, and I was not about to bind myself to this person just because he chose to sit down so early. I felt no obligation to sit down just because he has no one to talk to—it was his choice to sit down and not mingle. Instead of sitting down, I said something like, "Jake, great meeting you. I look forward to continuing a conversation with you, but I need to go meet _____ from company." I'll be back."

Next, I went up to a table of the company that I was interested in connecting with to discuss a question I had been thinking about. I introduced myself and shook hands with everyone who was seated at the table and heard them say their names. (No, I have not conquered how you remember the name of every person I meet—that is why contact cards are so important.)

Someone on LinkedIn said he goes to events and pretends he is the host of the event. Smiling when I read it, I realized that is what I do though I had not put any terminology around it. People appreciate anyone who can make a situation seem lighter or more interesting.

Hint: Make sure you have a big smile when you approach a table.

WHEN THE FORMAL PART OF THE MEETING STARTS:

You excuse yourself immediately from any conversation and head to your table. By now, the whole table will be full of participants. You slip into your seat, smile, and get there in time for people to introduce themselves.

Hint: Take out enough contact cards for everyone at the table, and pass them to the left. I can assure you no one will do it until you do, and all will be grateful they have the contact information of those at your table. There is bound to be great information surfacing during the course of the event.

I find it fascinating that rarely do people take notes during the course of a presentation. Personally, I cannot imagine not having a place to write an "aha" down. These "ahas" serve as ideas for my blog, useful website addresses or a quote might be something that I can use in my own Weekly Wisdom.

Hint: Keep a small notebook in your purse or briefcase. You can also download an app to your smart phone so you can capture the essence of what you are hearing and learning. Yes, I feel this is a good use of your smartphone at a meeting.

WHAT DO YOU DO AFTER CLOSING REMARKS ARE MADE?

By this time, you have been able to connect with many people at your table. Get up from the table and shake hands with all of the people that you can before they scoot out the door.

Hint: Schedule your time so that you have time to mingle after an event. People forget this time gives you opportunity to speak with the main speaker, or go up to someone who may have been mentioned during the course of the event. Let's say you learned a person received a major award. There is nothing better than being congratulated with a warm handshake and a smile.

FOLLOW-UP AFTER THE EVENT

See Chapter 10 on "Handwritten Notes are Very Much Appreciated."

IT'S THE LITTLE THINGS

1.   Go early to events and leave late.

2. Find yourself a table facing the podium, drop off your coat and belongings at your chosen space, and then mingle.

3. Go by yourself to events or make sure you do not sit with your colleagues that you see every day.

How Do You Start and Maintain a Conversation?

"Questions that work well to start conversations and questions to avoid."

You have perfected your handshake. You know what to do when you walk into a room. Now what? Time to begin a conversation.

In this chapter, you will be given many suggestions about how to start a conversation. One caveat: If you start a conversation and do not listen to the answer, you will find yourself lacking in the ability to carry on a meaningful conversation. Listening to the answer of a question is key. Recently, the late David Broder, a

noted American journalist and Pulitzer-Prize winning
columnist for **The Washington Post**, said, "Never
talk when it interferes with listening."

Too often, when a person is listening to someone, he
creates in his mind something he wants to say on a
particular subject. As a result, he may interrupt the
person speaking before he is finished. This is not a
way to build a relationship. In fact, it has the opposite
effect. The person may feel you are dismissing his
statement and conclude that you are not listening to
him, which may or may not be accurate.

While I am not one to focus on the negative, I feel it is
important that you, the reader, understands why
certain questions are better avoided when starting a
conversation.

HERE ARE SOME EXAMPLES:

"Hi. How are you?"

I always knew this question was not a good conversation starter. However, I didn't know why. Now I do.

A few years ago, when I was receiving radiation for breast cancer I stopped by my local grocery store. The impact of radiation cannot be truly described, and on this particular day, I was feeling particularly down. I walked into the fruit department and a young woman said, "Hi, how are you?" Instead of my normally chipper "Doing great", I replied, "Not very good."

The woman's head immediately dropped down and she busied herself with the task at hand. She did not utter another word. I said, "If you don't care, why did you ask?" She said, "The manager told us to ask people how they are." There was nothing more for me to say.

A month later, I had the opportunity to meet the regional manager of the same grocery chain. I told her about my experience and she said, "Corporate says we have to teach our staff to say to say 'Hi. How are you?' If they don't say it, and a mystery shopper comes along, staff will be written up." Hmmmm.

"What do you do?"

I am betting there is not a person reading this who has not found themselves between jobs or knows of someone who is without a job.

In the case mentioned above, each time the question is asked, "What do you do?" the person is reminded that he is not employed. Before you know it, a whole conversation revolves around how long he has been out of work. Let's just say asking this question is not the best way to create an upbeat, positive atmosphere.

NOW LET'S LOOK AT QUESTIONS THAT WORK WELL TO START A CONVERSATION

"What great thing happened to you recently?"

This is my favorite question and here's how I use it: As I approach someone, I reach out for a handshake, smile, and say, "Hi, I'm Kathy Condon." Tell me what great thing happened to you recently."

Ninety-eight percent of the time I will get a big smile, and the person will reply with a comment such as, "I just came out of a meeting where I closed a big deal",

"I just found out I am going to be a grandparent", "I just got back from NYC" or "Well I got up this morning so that means I'm still alive." (This answer automatically brings a smile to both of our faces!)

There are two reasons why this particular question works so well.

1. In order to answer the question, the person has to focus on something positive. So even if he has just had a big fight with his spouse, came from a downsizing meeting, or lost a major deal, your question takes him into a more positive territory.

2. If you listen to his answer, you immediately have the opportunity to ask him another question.

Yes, occasionally you will get a negative answer. Each time it has happened to me, the person obviously needed to talk about the negative issue. I listened, asked more questions, and steered him into positive territory.

When you are meeting new people, remember: You know everything you know—your goal is to learn about the other person.

"Great pen."

As I write this, I am smiling, for just recently this statement started a fascinating conversation with an accountant. I was missing a pen to sign my book for one of the participants in a class I had just conducted. A man turned to me and said, "Here, use this one."

I finished signing the book and was handing the pen back to him and I said, "Great pen." The man replied, "Thank you. I got this pen many years ago when I received my accounting degree. It has been around a long time." Before long, we were discussing his career in accounting, where his office was located, and his particular niche in the accounting field.

You would be amazed at how many professional men have very special pens. Unlike me, they manage to keep their pens for years. You can be pretty sure their special pen has a story about how it was acquired or why it is of such personal value to the owner.

Hint: When going to a professional meeting, put away the pen that you picked up in a hotel and pull out your classy pen. Believe it or not, the pen you use will be noticed immediately.

"Great tie."

I believe that there is a story about how a particular tie enters a man's life. I even made the statement in one of my seminars, telling my audience that saying, "Great tie" is a really good way to start a conversation with a man, because he will want to talk about his tie and how he got it.

A young man in the audience disagreed with me. He said, "There is no story behind the tie I am wearing. I went to the store, bought a new suit, and wanted a tie that would go with it. So I looked and looked with the clerk and we spied one on the mannequin and made the clerk take it down. That is how I got it."

At this point, the whole group was snickering. One of them piped up and said, "Gee, I guess your tie does have a story." My point was made.

"How do you like _____?" (This works well with electronic gadgets)

Whenever I ask this question, I do not have to worry about saying anything for the next ten minutes. People love to talk about the virtues and the failings a particular gadget! As always, in face-to-face networking, the key here is to keep listening. Asking this question is a great way to learn what the person is passionate about. You can ask someone which app he or she likes the best and you are then good for another 10 minutes of conversation.

"Great bracelet. Does it have a story behind it?"

My belief is that every piece of jewelry a woman wears has a story behind it. One time I had a room full of about 250 people. When I said, "Women have a story about their jewelry," a woman in the audience raised her hand and said, "Kathy, you are wrong, not all of us have stories about our jewelry. For example, this necklace is one that I just bought in Arizona because I collect turquoise jewelry—it has no story about it." Again, the audience started snickering and the woman realized that there was, indeed, a story about her necklace.

To continue that conversations we could have said such things as, "Jane, tell me about your collection.

How did you get started? How many pieces to you have? Do you collect necklaces?" Trust me, people love talking about their collections.

You goal is to keep asking questions and learning about the individual.

Hint: A young man said, "Kathy, we men have jewelry too. In fact, I am a barista and I wear this bracelet. I have had more women start conversations with me by asking me about my bracelet."

The key here is being sincere in ANY compliment that you give a person when you are starting a conversation. Do not say things you do not sincerely mean. For example, if a woman is wearing pin and you think it is one of the ugliest things you have ever seen, you can still start a conversations by saying "That is really an unusual pin."

YOU DO NOT TALK ABOUT BUSINESS

Some of you reading this might be thinking: "This personal stuff is okay, but "we are supposed to be networking. So, when do you bring up your business?" My quick reply is, "You don't."

Before your blood pressure starts to rise and you label this book as rubbish, let me reinforce some statements that I have made earlier in the book.

PEOPLE DO BUSINESS WITH PEOPLE THEY LIKE AND KNOW

One time, I went to an event at 7:30 a.m. and woman came up to me and said, "Hi Kathy, I am Angela, "What do you take for your health?" Since I hadn't had my coffee yet, I thought I had heard her wrong

and said, "What did you ask me?" She said, "What do
you take for your health?"

To say I had a negative reaction to this encounter,
would be putting it mildly. This woman was asking
me a personal question and she had absolutely no idea
who I was or knew anything about my current
circumstances.

At a networking event, your goal is to start a
conversation with a person and learn something about
him. I repeat, "You know everything you know." You
do not talk about business unless the person with
whom you are communicating asks you.

Chapter 9, The Power of Three, talks about how to
break away from conversations.

After the event, write a handwritten note, enclose your contact card, and set up a coffee date so you both can share what you do in your careers. That is when you start talking about your business.

IT'S THE LITTLE THINGS

1. Practice the question "What great thing happened to you recently?" with a sales clerk or one of your colleagues. Watch for the smiles—you'll quickly see why it is an effective question to ask.

2. Take notice of the way people approach you. Did it make you feel good? It is okay to "borrow" someone's opening question, if you believe it an effective way to start a conversation.

3. The goal is to make everyone with whom you meet feel important or significant.

NOTES

9

Contact Cards: Power of Three

"What is the goal for a one-hour event?"

You have just returned from a networking event and you empty your pockets of the contact cards you got at a networking event. If you are smart, there will only be three of them.

What are you talking about? I thought the goal was to acquire as many cards as possible at networking events. WRONG. Someone, somewhere, sometime ago started that myth. My view is that this approach is *not* the way to network and build relationships.

Let me give you a personal example. One evening I attended a grand opening of a business. It was a classy place and I was looking forward to connecting with community leaders. I was enjoying talking with someone I had just met, when the Master of Ceremonies announced to the group, "We are going to play a game to see who can get the most cards. These are the rules….."

I turned back to the person I was talking to person for it was the last thing I wanted to do was to collect cards at a fast pace. Suddenly a man appeared out of nowhere, interrupted our conversation, and said, "Where do you want to go on vacation?" Too surprised to think, I looked at him and just blurted out Belize. He said, "Great, can I have your card?" I gave it to him and he walked away. Huh?

This event happened three years ago. It is still vivid in my mind. I see this man repeatedly at events but to this day, I do not feel that we connect when we run into each other. He has never made an effort to carry on a real conversation with me. I cannot help but think the only reason he first introduced himself to me that night was so that he could win the grand prize for collecting the most business cards that evening.

THE GOAL OF A ONE-HOUR EVENT IS THREE CONTACT CARDS

The mere mention of a going to a networking event can panic an individual. After much research and questioning, I realize one of the reasons is that people "think" they have to meet many people at the event.

When I am speaking and training on my topic, Face-To-Face Networking is Dead. Wrong!" Participants are always surprised when I say, "You only want to acquire three cards in an hour."

This approach not only takes the pressure off, it helps you build stronger relationships. Why? You have a longer time to talk and get to know things about the person. Humans have an emotional need—they want to feel that they are significant or important. By taking time to talk with an individual and look him in the eyes, you are helping him feel he is the most important person in the room.

After you have spent some time with the individual, you can break away with statements such as:

"I promised myself I would meet three people tonight, I have two to go."

"Time for a refill."

"I want to be sure and thank the host for the great evening."

You can use any of these statements, or make up your own authentic one. At this point, you extend your hand for a firm handshake, use her, name, and then ask, "Do you have a contact card?"

I can assure you that people will not feel you are slighting them in any way if you ask for a contact card.

IT'S THE LITTLE THINGS

1. Make it a goal to meet three people at a one-hour networking event.

2. Keep your contact cards handy so it is easy to get them out of your purse or pocket.

3. Make a note on the back of the contact card that will trigger a reminder about the person or what he said—it will come in handy for the handwritten note you will be sending him.

10

Handwritten Notes are Very Much Appreciated

"What do you say on a handwritten note?"

People remember the days well when the mail carrier was admired and appreciated for he brought with him communication from loved ones. In his mailbag were letters that were not only touched by human beings, but often carried great joy, sorrow and our history. Letters were cherished pieces of communication and were often preserved in boxes that are still being found in attics today.

Technology is growing and *cursive handwriting,* defined by Webster's Dictionary as "handwriting that flows with the strokes of successive characters joined and the angles rounded" is no longer taught in the schools. Most communication tends to come through some form of technology—more specifically texting and emailing.

WHY DO HANDWRITTEN NOTES CREATE SUCH AN IMPACT?

When I open my email in the morning, it is not unusual for 150 emails to flow into my inbox. For those of you who work for a corporation, it is not unusual for there to be 250 emails or more for you to wade through as you start your day.

Now let's say there is a note from someone you met at a networking event in your email inbox. The sender writes, "I enjoyed meeting you." They might mention something about your conversation. In any case, you say to yourself, "That's nice," then immediately delete the email and move on to your list of waiting emails.

Now let's contrast that to when you receive a handwritten note in the mail with a stamp on it. You open it up, look at the front and then you read the message that someone has taken the time to write you. Notice how you are smiling—yes, it happens every time for this is not a routine occurrence. The sender made you feel significant or important—a rare feeling in the workplace today.

The next thing you might do is show your colleague the note. A conversation ensues about how nice it was of the individual to take the time to send it. Then the most interesting thing happens. You don't throw the note away. You might even tack it up on your office wall. The handwritten note has much more of a shelf life than an email or a text.

WHEN ARE HANDWRITTEN NOTES APPROPRIATE TO SEND?

Let me give you some examples:

- Congratulations to a person upon receiving an award.

- Congratulations for a news article which included a quote or picture of a person. Send the clipping so the recipient has extra copies to use as he may see fit.

- If an article has been published with your picture or quote, send a note to the reporter who wrote it. Just so you know, reporters rarely get a thank you note.

- Letting a new acquaintance you met at a networking event know that you are glad you met.

- Thanking a person for breakfast, lunch, happy hour, or dinner.

- Thanking a person for inviting you to a special event.

- Thanking a manager of a restaurant or hotel for extraordinary service or help.

- Thanking a person for giving you a great idea.

- Thanking a person for supporting you at a meeting.

- Thanking a person for helping you with your job
  search.

  My belief is that a handwritten note should go to
  every person who helps you in your search.

- Thanking a person after an interview.

Yes, I am recommending you send a handwritten note
instead of an email after an interview. At a technology
company, I conducted a survey of hiring managers.
There was 95% agreement that they would rather
receive a handwritten note. The trick is to get the note
to the hiring manager or the interviewing team within
48 hours—your thank you note could make the
difference in you being hired.

What other ideas do you have to add to this list?

WHAT DO YOU SAY IN THE HANDWRITTEN NOTES?

1. If you are writing someone after a networking event, be sure to start out with something like—"It was great meeting you at the Chamber of Commerce mixer Thursday night." You want to be sure the person remembers where you met.

2. Second sentence includes something personal you learned about them in your conversation. Example: "What a fortunate person you are, heading off to South Africa in a few days!"

3. Third sentence: "I'm putting your return date in my calendar—I'd like to sit down and have coffee with you so I will give you a call later in the month."

There is no need for more than three lines. I choose to sign it "With every good wish, Kathy." Choose a signature line that feels comfortable to you.

LAST BUT NOT LEAST:

ALWAYS include your contact card in the note. Brush aside the feeling that you are pushing your company. Instead, create the belief that you are making it easier for the person to get in touch with you.

Recently, I sent a note card with my contact card included. I got an email back from the recipient of the note that said, "I'm so glad you sent a contact card—now I have all of your information here in the office."

I have discovered that if I send a handwritten note I will get some kind of communication back, either in the form of an email, text, or phone call thanking me for the handwritten note 80 percent of the time.

WHAT TYPE OF NOTE CARD SHOULD I USE?

My personal preference is not to use one that says "thank you" on the front. Some how it feels like you are telling the person why you are writing before you get a chance to say it in your own words.

Blank note cards work great or you can have some made up with your name on them. My "business" note cards have my name on the front, and my contact information on the back. You just want to make sure there is nothing inside that will take away from your message.

In recent months, I have been stocking up on different cards with designs on the front of them. Some cards, for example, have more of an artistic flair for my contacts who I know appreciate the arts. Just make sure you do not buy note cards that are too "foo-foo." Handmade note cards are fine as long as they look classy.

I trust that I have made the case of why writing handwritten notes helps you stand out. We have gone back to adding the human touch to our communication. Get out your favorite pen and send someone a special note today.

IT'S THE LITTLE THINGS

1. Unlike email or text notes, handwritten notes are not immediately deleted—they are often saved.

2. When a person writes a note, they have to schedule the time, select the note, write the note, and then mail it. How can you not feel significant or important when you get such a note in the mail?

3. Since this is the longest chapter in the book, you can tell I believe the effort to write a handwritten note is more than worth it. It is an easy way to connect with a person and trust me: you will smile as you slip the note into the mail.

Notes

11

Why is it Important to Manage Information on Your Contacts?

"What do you do with the contact cards you received?"

Let me begin by saying that, "I am confident you have already sent a handwritten note to the person whose name appears on the contact card you have on your desk." Okay, I know some of you are squirming a bit. You not only did not send them a handwritten note, you cannot remember where you got the card or who the person was whose name appears on the card.

A REVIEW OF THE BASICS:

1. Write on the back of the card where you met the person and something about him or her.

2. If you promised you would send some something, make a notation on the card about that too.

3. Sit down and write a handwritten note and include:

    a. Where you met and when.

    b. Something you learned about the person. Example: Great to hear about your trip to South Africa. I am looking forward to having a cup of coffee with you in the near future.

    c. Enclose your own contact card so it makes it easy for the person to get in touch with you or pass your card forward.

WHAT DO YOU DO WITH THE CONTACT CARDS FLOATING AROUND ON YOUR DESK?

Recently, I had an abundance of contact cards on my desk. I found some of them stuck in between papers that were part of a project I was developing. I knew my ultimate goal was to get the information on the contact cards into my contact program. For now, I needed to put the cards in one place where I could easily find them.

Since I like to use household items for new purposes, I looked in a kitchen cupboard. I found a handcrafted pie pan by an artist that I knew when I was finishing my degree in St. Thomas, US Virgin Islands. Perfect.

I walked into my office, found the perfect place for the pie plate on my desk, and put all the wayward contact cards on the plate. Now, I not only enjoy the artwork, I feel so much more organized. I know exactly where to look for one of the latest cards I have received.

Notice I said, "Latest cards." The other cards that I have received over the years have been discarded after I have entered them into my contact program.

WHY DO I NEED A CONTACT PROGRAM?

The people you meet through your work, whether they are clients, vendors, or colleagues, are people in your network. I cannot stress enough the importance of keeping their contact information somewhere.

Why? For many of you reading this book, you know the feeling of having to leave a company – whether by choice or your own initiative. In some cases, you may have had to pack up your belongings and be on your way immediately.

You walk out the door for the last time. All of the sudden you realize, "I don't have the email addresses or phone numbers of the people in my work database." That is right; you have left a goldmine of information behind and this information will never be retrieved.

I cannot stress this enough. Make sure you have all your contacts information at your work and at home. This applies to hourly employees, all the way up to CEOS. Let me repeat: "Keep a duplicate set of your contacts at home."

I have spoken about this at trainings and speeches where high-level CEOs and company presidents attended. They have NEVER questioned me on this statement. I followed up the statement with, "These are people you have gotten to know. Of course, you are NEVER to use this list to say things about your past employer or send emails of any kind that would affect the business of the company you are leaving."

Not only did top executives in the audience not object, they knew they were hearing information that they needed to pay attention to for their own good. They are not protected any more than hourly or other salaried employees when it comes to loss of position or a job change.

My personal belief is that some kind of contact program is the key to effective networking. In addition, make sure the program is backed up. Your contacts are one of your most valuable assets for your business and personal life.

IT'S THE LITTLE THINGS

1. Keep your contact cards in some sort of container until you are able to enter them into your contact program.

2. Keep a list of your contacts at home and at the office.

3. Find a contact program that works well for you. The important thing is to have one.

Notes

Appendix

Traveling and Using Your Smartphone

For many of us, once we get on a train, bus, or plane we are ready to relax after frantically handling last minute details. We take a deep breath and check to see if we have everything handy for the length of our journey: Book? Got it. Eyeglasses? Check. A pen for underlining or making notes? Check. For those of us who are less fortunate, and not in first-class on trains and airplanes, a water bottle is essential. We're all set to go.

Recently, this was the scene as I was about to embark on a 3.5 hour train ride from Seattle, Washington to Vancouver Washington. The trip takes me along the

Hood Canal and on any given day, the scenery is spectacular. On this trip, my timing was such that that I would be able to watch the sunset over the Canal. What a special treat!

We hadn't yet pulled away from the station when a young woman in the seat in front of me started a phone conversation. I could hear every word she said. I convinced myself that she was just making a quick call to tell her Dad before the train pulled away from the station.

The train started its' journey and the sights of Seattle whizzed by my window. The young woman's conversation continued as she told her Dad about her first time in a casino and how she had won $16. She shared news about her new apartment, the job application she had put at the Cheesecake Factory (I can even tell which location) and how she wasn't sure about her new roommate.

She finished her conversation with her Dad and then called a girlfriend to discuss how she treated the new guy she met at special event in Seattle. Then, I had to hear about the casino, apartment, job etc....you get the picture.

Soon others were looking at me with sympathy. The man behind me asked the conductor if he could pass out earplugs. It soon was evident that EVERY person in the car was hearing every word of her conversation as well.

I tapped on the woman's shoulder and said, "Are you aware that everyone in this car has heard everything you have said on your phone calls?" She gave me a disgusted look, and then signed off on her phone call.

This isn't an isolated story. The same thing happens at airports in waiting rooms, on planes —especially if the is plane is delayed and sitting on the tarmac.

Travelers need to understand that most of the time "private conversations" are not private. If you need to make a phone call, look for an area that is away from the assembled crowd.

Notes

Notes

About the Author

Kathy Condon

As a certified Executive Performance Coach, I am driven by a distinct purpose to motivate others to achieve and contribute their full potential. My career involves traveling the world as an international speaker, executive coach, trainer, and award-winning published author.

Fortune 100 companies embrace my coaching style for the hallmark of my approach is one of listening closely, then introducing and utilizing tools that help the organization or employees with their communication issues.

My first book *"It Doesn't Hurt to Ask: It's All About Communication"* was recently named "Best Book Award Finalist by USA Book News." Whether you are a seasoned professional, a person graduating from college or about to graduate from high school, there are tools throughout this book that will serve you well. This is book is about stripping away the fluff and looking at the simple things you can do every day to raise your ability to communicate with others.

"Weekly Wisdom" is my Ezine that offers insights and thought-provoking comments about current events, business communication, and career issues. It is emailed to hundreds of people each week.

My learning never stops. I am frequently a participant or a presenter at international and national conferences, where I test my beliefs about networking and communication. These events serve as a resource for material that confirms and strengthen my belief that people learn and understand better if you support the statement you make with the "why" the suggestion or directive is being made.

I received my BA at the University of the Virgin Islands-St Thomas. I am certified in Performance Coaching, Certified in Interact—Personal Assessment Profile, Employer Retention Specialist Program, Globally Certified Career Facilitator and a graduate of Anthony Robbins Master University.

Vancouver, Washington has been my home for 26 years. I am the mother of two daughters, Kara Marie and Tami Louise. I am honored to have two son-in-laws and two grandchildren, Taylor and Juliette.

The visual arts and exploring what is around the corner renews me. Since I am so fortunate to have a career that does not feel like work, I have to actually put into my calendar when a day will be one detached from technology. So much to do, so few hours in the day—and most importantly, I love every minute of my days.

My Mission Statement:

"The purpose of my life is to cultivate and share wisdom. Enjoy soaring to new heights and increase the quality of day for myself and others."

Phone: (360) 695-4313

http://www.kathycondon.info

kathy@kathycondon.info

http://www.kathycondon.info/blog

Weekly Wisdom Ezine:
http://www.kathycondon.info/21201.html

WHAT PEOPLE ARE SAYING ABOUT

KATHY CONDON

"I've known Kathy for several years, having attended one of her workshops on networking when she just moved into consulting. Over the years, she has inspired me as well as become a constant source of tools to use in my professional network, whether it is face-to-face, over the phone, and by social networking.

She recently spoke to a group of technology professionals here. She has the gift to cross-occupational, gender or social boundaries to deliver an outstanding presentation with bags full of take away methods to use in the real world of networking and communicating with people in business and personal life.

If you have the opportunity to hear Kathy speak, take advantage of it. You will walk away more knowledgeable and wealthier."

Gary Perman
President
Perman Technical Search Group

"Recently, I asked Kathy Condon to guest speak for me at a "center of influence" networking event that I sponsored for a close knit professional group. Kathy cleared her calendar for this evening event. Because she did, the event turned out to be one of the most enjoyable opportunities to meet several new individuals on a very favorable basis. Kathy did a great job of breaking down barriers and making people laugh. She taught us how to shake hands the 'right way' and ask, 'What great thing happened to you recently?'

Kathy is so wonderful at helping people to understand how important it is to seek to understand first the needs of others!"

Kris L. Greene
Manager/Recruiter
County Financial

RADIO INTERVIEWS

"My experience booking Kathy Condon on radio recently has been wonderful. Kathy complies with all requests in a cooperative, timely, and professional fashion. She is a strong media guest and I would be happy to present her to future media outlets."

Maryanna
Publicist
Annie Jennings, PR

"I enjoyed my interview with Kathy because she listened to my needs and thoroughly understands her subject. She had so much good information to offer about networking, I asked her to come back. Her second show was a perfect fit with the first and generated favorable comments from listeners."

Will Kayos
The Real State of the Union, LLC

SPEAKING

"Kathy Condon provided insight related to communication and the subtle things we can do to improve our handshake and be memorable to the people with whom we interact. We appreciate that was very approachable and took times to shake hands, sign autographs, and answer questions our members had. She has a wonderful sense of humor and a commanding presence. Ms. Condon is dedicated to helping others achieve their personal best."

Pacific Northwest License Tax and Fraud
Association

"I recently had the pleasure of hearing Kathy speak at a conference. She has that rare presentation style that successfully combines good information, laughter, and audience participation. The rapt audience came away with a good set of tips on the art of networking,

as well as thought provoking ideas to explore both personally and in business."

Valerie Matta
VP Business Development
CareerShift, LLC

"Kathy Condon's back-to-basics approach to personal communication is refreshing and powerful. With so much emphasis on social media, emails and blogs, it's nice to know that the most successful communications are still those that go hand in hand with relationship building and an awareness of people's values, beliefs, and personal backgrounds."

Ken Cole
Manager of Public Affairs
Southwest Washington Health Systems

TRAINING

"I always enjoy attending Kathy's seminars. She is full of energy and real-life stories, which makes it easy to translate her ideas into my own environment. The most recent presentation on networking was especially helpful as I started a new career, which requires me to approach unfamiliar faces at events. Her back-to-basics communication and networking suggestions will help me to take the first step."

Susanne Cox
AmeriBen/Group

"Kathy's training is great! The tools she shares are practical and easy to implement. She brings energy to the group that motivates people to try new ideas and have a renewed excitement in their jobs."

Cyndi Bower, formerly with the State of California

EXECUTIVE COACHING

"If you are looking for an enthusiastic, relevant coach to improve your business, communication, sales, or marketing Kathy can bring you to a high functioning level. Kathy engages you with humor and practical tips that are easy to understand and apply."

Angela Brosius
Director
East Vancouver Business Association Community Affairs

"Kathy Condon has worked with one our clients and the feedback has been outstanding—strong upfront analysis of the areas for improvement, practical/usable advice and tools, and enjoyable personality. She really cares about the people she coaches!"

Tracy Peterkin
TJ and Associates

"Kathy's concrete and simplistic advice has made a world of difference to me both personally and professionally. By applying her tools and suggested techniques, I have gained confidence and purpose."

Lisa Gibert
President/CEO
Clark College Foundation

"Our family started our company 35 years ago. When we decided to build a new store, we knew we needed help deciding on an organizational structure and filling the various positions. We hired Kathy Condon who suggested an appropriate structure, interviewed our current staff, and helped us decide which person was appropriate for a given task. We asked our employees if they were ready to stretch and wanted to take an increasingly active role in the development of the company. Today, we are one of the leading music companies in the United States.

Kathy's facilitation changed our business for the better, and brought our business to a whole new level!"

Gayle Beacock
VP of Beacock Music Company

Sign up for *Weekly Wisdom*, Kathy's Ezine that helps you focus your week!

http://www.kathycondon.info/21201.html

Weekly Wisdom

"Surround yourself with talented people."

Unknown Author

By now you understand that great leaders hire people who are better than them in certain areas. Great leaders know they cannot be good at everything.

Are you surrounding yourself with people that are better than you?

www.kathycondon.info
Phone: (360) 695-4313
www.kathycondon.info/blog
linkedin.com/in/kathycondon

It Takes a Village to Produce a Book

This is my second book. The first one is *"It Doesn't Hurt to Ask: It's All About Communication."* Starting out, I thought this would be so much easier since I know what to do this time around. However, the two final months before this book arrived were, once again, busy with things that had to be done. When you hear about authors becoming a hermit just before the birth of their book, be understanding for there appears to be no way around the last flurry of activity—especially if you are self-publishing.

The final edit needed to be done, readjusting of the cover design to include the new title, getting the ISBN number assigned, barcode made, finalize what will be on the back cover and, of course setting the cover and pages for printing.

The people in the production of this book know what is involved and they know I am grateful. However, I want to publicly thank them for their time, expertise and sense of real caring for me as an author. We worked to make this best book on face-to-face networking one that will continue to serve individuals in the future.

The material in here is timeless for we have refrained from using links to social media sites. This book is about relationships---just like the kind that helped me so much in the production of this book.

Janet Clemmerson, Cover Design

Janet is my sister. She lives and works in Mission, Texas. She has TESOL Certificate, which enabled her to teach English for one year in Beijing, China. She will now be heading to Columbia to use her skills.

When deadlines were short or a plea from me for one last check of something, Janet was there for me. No one could ask for a better sister than me. She tirelessly readjusted the cover for the new title. As you will note, this book is my second in a series on "It's All About Communication."

Roselyn Hall, Creative Director

 Rosie is a friend of mine and lives here in Vancouver, Washington. Rosie came to me and asked if she could help draw and find additional drawings to fit the subjects of the various chapters for the first book. Since the first book was named "Best Book Finalist by USA Book News," I knew I had the formula for success.

Once I officially decided to write this book, I called Rosie and asked her again, if she would be part of the project. She said, "Certainly. Just send me the chapters when they are done so I can come up with a drawing that is appropriate."

Rosie is an amazing entrepreneur, who has owned and operated a commercial janitorial service since 1979. Rosie is not slowing down and has on her bucket list an extended stay in Italy—I know she will make it happen.

Rosie can be reached at: Rosie@t00@comast.net

Holly Paige

I met Holly through a mutual friend. It wasn't long before I learned Holly is terrific at recording stories and a talented copywriter. She stuck by me through thick and thin on this project.

"Thank you Holly for your thoughtful and professional copy editing and proofreading expertise."

Holly can be reached at: holly@waveonegroup.com

Task Jeanie LLC, Book Formatting

Jeanie, thank you for your professionalism, sense of humor and timely delivery of product.

Task Jeanie LLC offers extensive virtual administrative support services to help clients meet their goals. By delegating tasks to Jeanie, clients save time, free up resources, cut costs and easily meet deadlines. Visit www.taskjeanie.com to learn more about the services Jeanie offers.

Finally, a special thank you to all my friends who supported me in this endeavor. There were times I had to say no to an outing, canceling at the last minute due to a deadline. Your understanding is appreciated more than you know.

Interested in Ordering More of Kathy's Products?

I trust you enjoyed the journey provided by this book.

Would you like to order additional copies for gifts for your friends and colleagues? We are happy to handle your order directly!

As noted on the form on the next page, you can also order the Second Edition of Kathy's first book: *"It Doesn't Hurt to Ask: It's All About Communication."* Additionally, you can purchase her two CD set entitled *"It's the Little Things – Connect with People",* which includes most of the tools and suggestions written in this book.

Simply complete the following order form, and send with your check or credit card information to the address listed on the form. You can order online on her website at www.kathycondon.info.

In the event you would like your order shipped directly to the recipient of your generosity – be sure to provide their address as well.

Please call (360) 695-4313 for quantity discounts.

KC SOLUTIONS Order Form

BILLING INFO:

Name:

Street:

City, State, Zip:

SHIP TO (if different than billing):

Name:

Street:

City, State, Zip:

Email:

QTY	PRODUCT	EA	TOTAL
	Face-To-Face Networking: It's All About Communication	$15.95	
	It Doesn't Hurt to Ask: It's All About Communication	$13.95	
	It's the Little Things - 2 CD Set	$10.00	
	Purchase all three	$35.00	
	WA State shipment add 8.2% sales tax		
	Free Shipping & Handling!		
		TOTAL	

Credit Card Info

Type	Number	Exp.	Sec. Code

Signature

Checks: Send to
KC Solutions
5535 E. Evergreen Blvd. #7102
Vancouver, WA 98661

This book is dedicated to my one-room schoolteacher, Mrs. Jensen. To honor her memory, I am donating a portion of the sale of each book to:

Harney Elementary School
3212 E. Evergreen Blvd.
Vancouver Washington 98661

The fund is designated for materials and resources for the teachers in this school.